NVQ Assessment To The A1 Standards

....

Piers Liron RDN FIVA(V)

© Piers Liron 2003

ISBN 0-9546427-0-8

First Published in 2003

Published in Great Britain by:

Piers Liron

A catalogue record for this book is available from the British Library.

Printed in Great Britain by

Biddles Ltd
Kings Lynn, Norfolk

E-Book distributed by

Marc Liron

Dedication

To John Sanderson who has been my teacher, mentor and NVQ assessor, and first taught me the true meaning of quality in NVQ assessment.

To my work colleagues who started the journey with me on the road to NVQ enlightenment and shared the ups and downs of creating an NVQ centre based on quality staff, quality assessment and quality procedures.

Oggy for making life easier by the joys of Hyper-Linking!

Mandy for getting us through the tough periods with humour.

Amanda for sharing the same enthusiasm which has driven our loved ones crazy.

Richard for the tremendous administrative support.

Pidders for helping me get the job which has resulted in this book and a lifetime ambition of becoming a published author.

And finally for my wife Lesley and daughter Simoné for believing in me.

About the Author

Piers Liron is a qualified Dental Nurse who is currently working as an NVQ Scheme co-ordinator for Oral Health Care, and Assesses and Internal Verifies Oral Health Care, Key Skills, Business Administration and the Assessor and Internal Verifier Awards. He has also recently started to work with an Awarding Body as an External Verifier.

He has lectured on the subject of NVQs and worked as a consultant to NVQ centres in training Assessors and setting up NVQ Schemes.

It has been said he is incredibly passionate about Dental Nurses and to prove the point he recently married one!

This book has also seen him realise his ambition to become a published author

Contents

Preface

This book was written to help Assessors carry out assessment on their candidates in line with the current A1 Unit – Assess candidates using a range of methods.

It can be used by people who are working towards this qualification to help them understand the process in clear, understandable English rather than the sometimes heavy going NVQ jargon.

It is also designed to be used by those Assessors who qualified under the previous D32 & D33 Units, to help them confirm they are assessing to the new A1 standards.

But most importantly it is there to help any Assessor, new or old, as a reference book as and when they require it.

The processes are all written in a logical and simple step by step guide that can be followed with ease. Where a paragraph has reference to the A1 Unit Standards, you will see the Performance Criteria indicated in brackets at the end (e.g. A1.1.a = Unit A1. Element 1. Performance Criteria a.

Each stage of assessment is explained and also lists the documents and forms you will need.

Examples of the forms are at the back of the book in the Annexes, some of which include completed examples. These forms are not intended to be represented as the forms that should be used, but rather to show the reader what information should be contained on each form (names, dates, location, signatures and other information) in accordance with the A1 Unit standards.

These may be used, however, in the first instance you should check with your Internal Verifier to confirm what paperwork they require you to use.

After the stages of assessment are explained there are sections on the different methods of assessment you can use and the quality checks that should be made to ensure they produce acceptable evidence.

Also contained are sections on Particular/Special Assessment Requirements, Candidate Appeals Procedure, Assessor Questions and Simulation Requests. All of these are mentioned throughout the stages of assessment and referred to if the assessor needs to consider them.

This book is used by myself and the assessors in my centre to ensure we keep our assessments to the highest quality.

If you feel this book could be improved in any way or you wish to make any comments, the author would be delighted to hear from you.

It only remains for me to wish you well in your assessing and hope this book will be of long and valued use to you.

The Initial Interview

This applies to a brand new candidate starting an NVQ, as well as to a candidate who has been working towards their NVQ and you have just taken over as their designated work based assessor.

The purpose of this interview is to find out what prior experience and qualifications the candidate has with regard to the NVQ they are undertaking. This will establish what areas the candidate may already have evidence for.

You will need:

1 x Step-by-step guide for Candidate Initial Interview *(Annex A)*

The procedure:

1.   Explain to the candidate that this is an informal fact finding interview to determine what previous NVQ/Topic area qualifications/experience they have.

2.   Complete the candidate name and contact details.

3.   Ask the candidate if they hold any NVQ qualifications, if so note them in the NVQ qualifications box. This is important as NVQs are designed to be transferable qualifications, for example every NVQ has a unit on Health and Safety. *(A1.1.f)*

4.   Ask the candidate if they have any other qualifications in the topic area of the NVQ they are undertaking. For example has the candidate gained a non-NVQ qualification for either the full job they do, or for some of the tasks they now undertake in their present job role. This may take some digging by yourself so you must be fully aware of the NVQ units open to the candidate, as they may not realise something they have could be relevant. If so then note them down in the Topic Area qualifications box. *(A1.1.f)*

5.   Ask the candidate if they have any experience with NVQs. They may not have a full NVQ but may have previously started one and have an understanding of the NVQ process. This will help with deciding the level of support your candidate requires from you. If so note this down in the NVQ prior experience box. *(A1.1.f)*

6.   Ask the candidate if they have any previous experience in the topic area of the NVQ they are undertaking. For example has the candidate worked in a similar job previously, or a job that included some of the tasks they now undertake in their present job role. If so then note them down in the Topic Area prior experience box. *(A1.1.f)*

7.   If the candidate has no previous qualifications or experience then you must annotate the relevant box with "NIL", just to confirm that it has been looked at. *(A1.1.f)*

8.   Finally you must determine whether the candidate as any Particular Assessment Requirements (PARs), sometimes called Special Assessment Requirements, and note them. **READ THE SECTION ON PARTICULAR ASSESSMENT REQUIREMENTS**, this section will inform you of exactly what a PAR is and the action to take if it is discovered that your candidate has any. *(A1.1.g)*

9.　　If so, you will need to complete a PAR form *(Annex B)* and send it to the Internal Verifier. This will ensure that your candidate is not disadvantaged in any way, and all candidates with a similar PAR are treated the same. *(A1.1.g)*

Next Step

You now have all the background information you need to start raising your assessment plans.

By completing this initial interview form and having it with you whenever you raise an assessment plan, you have a constant reminder of areas of evidence that may already exist. This will save the candidate time and effort in repeating areas they are already competent in, and allows you to be sure that you are raising fair assessment plans. *(A1.1.f)*

Once this interview is completed and any PAR action has been taken, you are ready to start an assessment planning session.

Assessment Planning Session

Now you have a completed Initial Candidate Interview, you should have a fair idea of where you should start assessing your candidate against the NVQ. This will be the area of the NVQ that your candidate has previous qualifications or experience, you just need to decide which unit you are going to start with.

Once you have decided which unit, you **must** take time to read this thoroughly so you have a full understanding of what you are going to plan to assess.

This includes all the performance criteria, range or scope, and knowledge statements. You must also read the **Guidance Notes** for each unit. This will let you know if there are any special assessment requirements which could dictate what method of assessment has to be used or cannot be used. It might also inform you of a requirement for more than one piece of evidence, ie show competence 3 times.

Should you have any trouble understanding any part of the unit, be it a performance criteria, range or scope statement, a knowledge statement or evidence requirement, you must seek advice from the Internal Verifier. *Do Not* guess or assume, if anything is unclear complete the Assessor Question Form at *Annex C,* and send it to the Internal Verifier immediately.

Do not attempt to plan an assessment for anything you have written to the Internal Verifier about, until you have received the reply. This will ensure that it is done correctly first time and does not need repeating, as this is unfair on your candidate.

Once you are confident you understand the unit/s to be assessed, you are ready to sit down with your candidate and commence the planning session. An example of a **completed Assessment Plan/Feedback Form can be found at *Annex E*.**

<u>**You will need**</u>:

1 x Completed Aide Memoir for Candidate Initial Interview
1 x Assessment Plan/Feedback Form (***Annex D***)
1 x Copy of the NVQ Standards you are going to assess
1 x Notes you have made on the unit/s to be assessed

<u>**Procedure**</u>:

1.   Ensure the candidate feels relaxed and is aware that this session is to agree an area of the NVQ to be assessed.

2.   Explain which area you think they are ready to be assessed for, and discuss with the candidate the reasons for this. Obtain their agreement that they feel ready to be assessed in this area. *(A1.1.a)*

3.   Using the completed Aide Memoir for Candidate Initial Interview, discuss with the candidate any areas of Accreditation of Prior Learning or Experience that may be relevant to unit/s you are going to assess. This will give you a clear indication of what has potentially already been achieved by the candidate, leaving you with remaining performance criteria, range/scope and knowledge statements that will require evidence by

© Piers Liron

other methods of assessment, taking into account any Particular Assessment Requirements. *(A1.1.c) (A1.1.d) (A1.1.f)(A1.1.g)*

4.   Take the Assessment Plan/Feedback Form *(Annex D)* and complete one of the boxes in the top left hand corner (Initial or Review). It will be an initial plan if this is the first time you have planned to look at a particular area, and a review if you are having to re-assess an area due to a Not Yet Competent decision being given at a previous assessment.

5.   Place the number 1 in the top right hand corner assessment plan No box if it is the first plan raised (or the next number if not the first plan raised). Numbering the plans allows them to be filed in the candidate's portfolio in numerical order, which should also therefore be in chronological order.

6.   Complete both your name and the candidate's names in the relevant boxes so that it is clear to all who this plan has been raised for. Remember both the Internal Verifier and External Verifier will be looking at these as part of their checks.

7.   Enter into the Qualification box the title or abbreviation of the NVQ the candidate is working towards.

8.   Enter into the Unit/s box, the Unit Numbers of the NVQ you are assessing. This allows for a clear indication as to which part of the qualification is going to be assessed.

9.   Ensure your candidate has a clear understanding of the unit/s they will be assessed against, then discuss with them the most practicable, cost/time effective way the assessment will take place. Read the guidance notes of the unit/s as this will give you an idea of the likely work activities that could be used for evidence. Remember to always check the Evidence Requirements section of the Unit/Element to see if there is a specific method that should be used, or should not be used. *(See section on Methods of Assessment) (A1.1.c)(A1.1.d)*

10.   In the column marked Elements, place the element number, performance criteria, range/scope, knowledge statements you are going to assess. These can all be on one row or you may wish to use separate rows for some or all parts of each section. See the **completed example of an Assessment Plan/Feedback Form (*Annex E*)**.

11.   To the right of this box is the section that you indicate if the planned assessment is going to be naturally occurring or a simulation, you will need to delete as appropriate. This is important as some qualifications do not permit simulated evidence to be used. *(See Simulation in Methods of Assessment Section and Simulation Request Section)*

12.   In the column marked method of assessment place a tick against the 1st method you have chosen to use to assess your candidate, ensuring you have confirmed with the candidate that there are no Particular Assessment Requirements that would affect which methods you chose. *(A1.1.g)*

13.   Now go to the column marked Evidence to be Provided and name the exact piece of evidence to be provided ie the name of a certificate, where questions are coming from, name of the process that is going to be observed or the name of any NVQ Centre provided tasks or projects.

14.   Place a tick in the box at the right of the evidence if the evidence is of a sensitive or confidential nature, i.e. medical in confidence, company confidential material, restricted management etc. You will then need to complete the box marked Details of how Confidential Information or Sensitive Issues will be dealt with, ensuring you give full details of how this information will be protected, but at the same time allow for valid assessment to take place. If in any doubt you should contact your Internal Verifier. *(A1.1.i)*

15.   Repeat this process for any other methods of assessment you intend to use. **You should always use assessor-devised questions as a secondary method of assessment**. This allows you to ask questions on the spot to clarify any points or cover any performance criteria, range/scope, knowledge that ends up not being covered by the other pieces of evidence you have planned to use. It is important to remember that you cannot ask the candidate questions at the judgement session if you have not agreed it with your candidate on the assessment plan. An example of a generic question/answer sheet can be found at *(Annex F)*. *(A1.1.c)(A1.1.d)(A1.1.e)*

16.   These columns are there so both you and the student know exactly what is going to happen and who is doing what. *(A.1.1a)(A1.1.b)(A1.1.c)(A1.1.d)*

17.   Now you need to complete the section underneath with the name and contact details of anyone who is going to be involved during the assessment process other than yourself and your candidate, or someone who is involved in providing evidence for the candidate. This could include:

      a.   Anyone who will be present in the area of an observation of a process, such as work colleagues, customers, patients etc.

      b.   Person providing witness testimony for a candidate.

You will need to confirm with any other individual what is required of them and offer them the support they may need for their involvement. This information is also required should the Internal Verifier need to contact them as part of their Quality Sampling Checks. *(A.1.1.h)*

18.   You now need to discuss with the candidate when an appropriate time would be to carry out this assessment plan. You will need to take into account the time it will take your candidate to get certain pieces of evidence like witness testimonies, or the time you need to put together question banks. Also when it would be convenient to carry out any observation in the workplace that you may need to get approval from the candidates line manager etc. *(A1.1.k)*

19.   Now in the When and Where you will Assess/Review section put the date, time and location (ie name of room, building, location etc) of when and where you are going to carry out this assessment. Never leave this section uncompleted as it can always be amended if your candidate needs more or less time to gather the required evidence or to arrange any observations etc. *(A.1.1.L)*

20.   Run through the plan again with the candidate to ensure their full understanding of what has been planned for the assessment, ask them if they have any questions regarding what has been discussed and agreed or what is due to happen during the next session. Confirm that if any disagreements between the Assessor and the Candidate occur during the Assessment session on how the assessment is being carried out or the competence

decision made, then in the first instance you will discuss it with them. If they are still unhappy then they should use the Candidate Appeals Procedure, **(See Section on Candidate Appeals Procedure)**, and get them to complete a Candidate Appeal Form, a copy of which can be found at *Annex G*. *(A1.1.b)*

21.   One last part of the form to action is the Yes/No check box to indicate if there were any difficulties experienced during the planning session. These could be interruptions, disagreements between candidate/assessor etc. If yes then give full details in the section provided.

22.   If the candidate is happy and fully agrees with the assessment plan then get them to sign and date at the bottom of the form, then do so yourself. Ensure you retain a copy of this plan for your records and the candidate puts the original in their NVQ Portfolio in the correct section. *(A1.1.a)*

23.   If the candidate does not fully agree with the assessment plan and you cannot sort it out by a face to face discussion then you should refer the candidate to use the candidate appeals procedure, **(See Section on Candidate Appeals Procedure)**, and get them to complete a Candidate Appeal Form, a copy of which can be found at *Annex G*.

Next Step

Having followed all of the above process you will have carried out an assessment planning session in accordance with the requirements of the NVQ Assessor qualification *(Unit A1)* and the requirements of your NVQ Centre.

You can now proceed with the Assessment at the agreed time and place. However should you or the candidate need to change the arrangements for carrying out the Assessment, you must both agree to the amendments and change the details on your own, and the candidates, Assessment Plan/Feedback Form.

Assessment/Judgement of Evidence Session

The Assessment/Judgement of Evidence Session is where you carry out what you have planned to do on your assessment plan.

You may not assess or judge any evidence, including asking questions, if it is not on the assessment plan you raised at the planning session. You may however add to this assessment plan when you first sit down with your candidate and review the plan prior to commencement.

You will need:

1 x Assessment Plan/Feedback Form (**Annex D**)
1 x Questions form (**Annex F**) if you have planned to use oral or written questions
1 x Relevant Observation Forms provided by the NVQ Centre, or Generic Observation
    Form (**Annex H**), if observation has been planned for
1 x Copy of the Standards you are going to assess
1 x Notes you have made on the unit/s to be assessed

Procedure:

1.   Sit down with the candidate and review the plan with them, confirming they have brought any evidence with them that you requested at the planning session, and that they are still happy for the assessment to take place. *(A1.2.a)*

2.   Confirm their understanding of what is about to happen, and allow them to ask any questions to clarify any areas of concern they may have, ensure you have taken into account any Particular Assessment Requirements. *(A1.2.f)*

3.   You will now carry out the judgement of each piece of evidence in accordance with the guidelines contained in the chapter on **Methods of Assessment**.

4.   Firstly ask to see any Accreditation of Prior Learning/Experience (Certificates) if this has been planned for. This should be the first type of evidence judged to ensure that all previous achievements by the candidate are taken into consideration before using other types of evidence. *(A1.2.b)*

5.   Next ensure the candidate has brought along any Witness Testimonies, products etc requested on the Assessment Plan. If observation of the candidate was planned for , this should be done first along with any associated questioning. The candidate can then return to their normal work activities while you take the time required to judge other pieces of evidence. *(A1.2.e)*

6.   Next you should look at the remaining evidence you agreed with your candidate on the Assessment Plan. Ensure you judge each piece of evidence thoroughly to ensure it is Valid, Authentic, Current, Sufficient and Safe/Sensitive as directed in the chapter on **Methods of Assessment.** *(A1.2.a)(A1.2.c)(A1.2.d)(A1.2.g)*

7.   Once you have judged a piece of evidence and decided on where competence has been achieved you will need to annotate this on the Assessment Plan/Feedback Form (**Annex D**). *(A1.2.i)*

8.   Put the date you are judging the evidence in the Review Date box.   The Remarks box is where you are going to give your judgement decisions and other comments. Firstly, start with making comments on:

    a.   Any evidence that was not provided and why, giving positive feedback to the candidate to advise them to bring everything you agreed on the plan. *(A1.2.h)(A1.2.i)*

    b.   Any problems that you had with location, time etc.

9.   Now write in the name of the first piece of evidence, (eg witness testimony from....., observation of........, question bank etc) and underline it. Underneath it list which Unit, Element, Performance Criteria, Range Statements and Knowledge Statements you are giving Competence for, see example at ***Annex E. (A1.1.m) (A1.2.i)***

10.   Should you find that the evidence is not sufficient to give a competent decision for all or some of the Performance Criteria, Range and Knowledge, you need to explain fully in writing to the candidate why this is the case. *(A1.1.m) (A1.2.h)*

11.   If you encounter any difficulty in judging a piece of evidence and feel unable to judge it accurately then you need to refer the piece of evidence to your Internal Verifier for clarification. *(A1.2.j)*

12.   Repeat this for every piece of evidence you had agreed on the assessment plan, even if you do not need to use it or it was not judged to give any evidence at all, you still need to make these comments so the candidate has a comprehensive feedback. Use as much space as you require using a separate sheet of paper if necessary. *(A1.1.m) (A1.2.h) (A1.2.i)*

13.   Do not forget to annotate each actual piece of evidence as directed by the **Methods of Assessment** section, to confirm the relevant checks have been made to ensure each piece of evidence is Valid, Authentic, Current, Sufficient and Safe. *(A1.2.d)*

14.   Now you need to give written instructions to the candidate to enter these pieces of evidence in their NVQ Portfolio evidence section, then cross-refer them where you have given competent decisions onto the evidence profile sheets (see example at ***Annex I***) for each element or set of knowledge statements. *(A1.2.i)*

15.   Finish off with a boosting comment of some kind to encourage the candidate, then tell them what is to be the next action, either review the assessment plan to gather new evidence to cover any areas where they were Not Yet Competent, or which part of the NVQ you suggest should be next for assessment.

16.   Now you need to make a note at the top if all the PCs, Range and Knowledge Statements were met that you had planned for on the assessment plan. There are 3 boxes, one for each, and you need to cross out the N (no) to show if all were met from what you had planned on the assessment plan, or the Y (yes) if not all that was planned was met by the evidence. *(A1.2.i)*

Next Step

Having followed all of the above process you will have carried out an Assessment/Judgement of Evidence session in accordance with the requirements of the NVQ Assessor qualification *(Unit A1)* and the requirements of your NVQ Centre.

Once you have completed the Assessment Plan/Feedback form and annotated each piece of evidence correctly, you are ready to start the feed back session with your candidate.

Next Step

Feedback Session

The feedback session is important to ensure that the candidate knows where they have been made competent and why, and where competence wasn't achieved and why.

It also allows for the candidate to discuss any areas of the assessment process with you and therefore ensures the candidates full understanding of the assessment process and the decisions made.

The feedback session does not have to take place directly after the judgement session, as you may wish to clarify or investigate something in depth before you can make a decision, but it should be as soon as possible. *(A1.3.a)*

<u>**You will need**</u>:

1 x Assessment Plan/Feedback Form *(Annex D)* completed at the judgement session
1 x Copy of the Standards you are assessing
All relevant evidence provided by yourself and the candidate.

<u>**Procedure**</u>:

1.	Ensure the candidate feels relaxed and is aware that this session is to provide them with feedback on your assessment decisions, informing them of where they have achieved competence or not achieved competence and why. It is also to allow them to ask questions and clarify any points they may have on your assessment decisions. *(A1.3.e)*

2.	Go through your Assessment Plan/Feedback Form explaining all you have written down, allowing for the candidate to ask questions at each point. Always ask them if they have understood what you have written and discussed. *(A1.3.b) (A1.3.c) (A1.3.e)*

3.	If the candidate is unhappy with any aspect of your assessment decisions, discuss this with them to try and resolve their concern. If the candidate is still unhappy refer them to use the candidate appeals procedure, **(See Section on Candidate Appeals Procedure)**, and get them to complete a Candidate Appeal Form, a copy of which can be found at *Annex G*. *(A1.3.g)*

4.	Once you have finished going through the Feedback/Review form, date and sign at the bottom then get the candidate to sign the form. *YOU MUST NOW PHOTOCOPY THE ASSESSMENT PLAN/ FEEDBACK FORM AND FORWARD TO THE NVQ CENTRE IMMEDIATELY,* this is required to ensure the candidates' records held by the NVQ centre are always up to date with the candidates' progress. Also should the candidate lose their NVQ Portfolio the NVQ centre has a record of the assessment decisions made, this will allow negotiation with the External Verifier that could allow the centre records to be duplicated and given back to the candidate without the need for the candidate to repeat all the work that has been lost. Now you can give the candidate the original Feedback/Review form and ensure you have directed them to put the form in the relevant section of their NVQ portfolio. *(A1.4.a) (A1.4.c) (A1.4.d)*

5.   Give the candidate the evidence you have judged and direct them to enter it in the evidence section of their portfolio. Remind them to number each piece of evidence and cross-refer it on the evidence profile sheets (see example at **Annex I**) for each element or set of knowledge statements.

6.   If full competence was not gained then you will need to raise a new Assessment Plan/Review form to cover the Performance Criteria, Range and Knowledge Statements competence wasn't given for. These should have been clearly stated in the written and verbal feedback to the candidate. **(A1.3.d)**

7.   If the candidate has gained full competence for all the Elements, PCs, Range etc on the Assessment Plan then return it to the candidate and direct them to place it in the relevant section of their NVQ Portfolio.

8.   When full competence is gained you will need to sign off each element on the evidence profile sheet (**Annex I**). Remember it is not just about ensuring there is a piece of evidence for each Performance Criteria/Range Statement (Scope)/Knowledge Statement, but you must also ensure that the Evidence Requirements have been met to. This could be using specific methods of assessment or the amount of evidence that should be produced.

9.   When a **Full Unit** has been completed you need to sign the Unit off on the Summary of Achievements at the front of the candidate's portfolio.

10.   You now need to go back to the **Assessment Planning Session** and start again. This will be to either provide more evidence for the areas given as not yet competent, or to start a new area of their NVQ. **(A1.3.d) (A1.3.f)**

Methods of Assessment

There are various methods of assessing your candidates' competence against the NVQ standards. Sometimes these will be dictated in the Evidence Requirements section of the Element or Unit, otherwise it is down to the Assessor and candidate to agree the most suitable opportunity.

Listed below are the methods open to you and the quality assurance checks you will need to make for each to ensure they are:

Valid - Is the evidence to be produced relevant to the Unit/Element to be assessed.

Authentic - Can the evidence to be produced be attributed as the candidates own work.

Current - Is the evidence to be produced currently showing the candidates competence at the Unit/Element to be assessed.

Sufficient - Will the evidence to be produced be sufficient to cover fully each Performance Criteria/Range Statement (Scope)/Knowledge Statement.

Sensitive - The evidence does not contain any sensitive restricted details or information such as Medical-in-Confidence, Contractual, Company-in-Confidence or information that is covered by the Data Protection Act and Access to Health Records Act.

Remember if you have any doubts about which method to use, or how to use a specific method, you should write to the Internal Verifier using the Assessors Question Form (**Annex C**).

Direct Observation

This method requires the assessor to watch the candidate physically performing the Performance Criteria/Range Statements (Scope)/Knowledge Statements. This can be either in the natural performance of their job (Naturally Occurring) or by arranging a Simulation (**if allowed** – see the Evidence Requirements for each Element).

The assessor is responsible for providing the candidate with written evidence detailing what the candidate was observed doing. This can be either by using pre designed Observation Reports provided by the NVQ Centre, or using the blank observation form at **Annex H**.

By using **Annex H** you can complete the areas you are looking to assess on the lines 1 to 6, thus giving you a checklist of what needs to be observed. These can be the exact Performance Criteria or an amalgamation of Performance Criteria, Range Statement and Knowledge Statement.

This is incredibly helpful to the student/assessor and the Internal/External Verifiers when the evidence is being cross-referred. Each PC, Range/Scope and Knowledge statement can then be easily identified without the need to wade through pages of written text.

Once the specific comment has been observed you can initial the box to the right hand side to confirm you have viewed this. If any of these comments are not observed then you can put a line through the initial box. If the candidate is observed performing but not to the required standard then you can place the capital letters **NYC** for Not Yet Competent.

The feedback/comments box is there for you to expand on this checklist, giving a clear picture on what was exactly seen by the assessor. Or you will need to expand on why an area was not observed, or explain what was wrong with the candidates performance that you did not deem it up to standard and Not Yet Competent. Leaving this area blank or failing to expand on what was seen during the observation will lead to the evidence being deemed insufficient.

The question boxes are designed for assessor-devised questions, either written or oral, that you may need to put to the candidate to clarify any area of the observation. You must always record any questions and answers put to your candidate.

Finally at the end of the observation you must date and sign the form at the bottom. You will need to get the candidate to sign the form at the Feedback Session. If you encounter any difficulty in judging the evidence competent/not yet competent then you should write to the Internal Verifier using the Assessors Question Form (**Annex C**).

Valid	-	Ensure that you only comment on the areas listed on your observation form, which should be exactly what you agreed with the candidate on the Assessment Plan.
Authentic	-	As this has been seen by the Assessor it can be attributed as the candidate's own work.
Current	-	This is shown by the competent decision made by the Assessor.

Sufficient - Ensure that each Performance Criteria/Range Statement (Scope) /Knowledge Statement that you are assessing can clearly be identified *IN FULL* on the observation form. If not then use the question section or a question form (*Annex F*) to record any questions you need to ask to supplement the observation report to be able to give a full competence decision for each Performance Criteria/Range Statement (Scope)/Knowledge Statement.

Sensitive - Always ensure that no information is recorded that could lead to the identification of specific customers, work colleagues or patients. These people should only be identified only if:

i)	absolutely necessary to validate the evidence.
ii)	the permission of the individual has been sought and obtained.
iii)	They are registered on the Witness List in the candidate's portfolio.

Also ensure no privileged/confidential/restricted information is recorded. If in any doubt always double check with the candidates line management to ensure no breach of the Companies Security Protocols, Data Protection Act / Access to Health Records Act etc.

Witness Testimony

Any individual considered to be competent (ie have relevant qualifications or experience) in the work activities which a candidate is being assessed on, can be requested to provide a witness testimony to confirm the candidate can and has been working to the required standards.

These can be used when having difficulty in directly observing a candidate's performance yourself. The witness either writes up their comments in a letter format or uses the pre-designed observation forms provided by the NVQ centre.

Remember that this will not count as observation as only an NVQ Assessor can produce direct observation evidence. Therefore ensure you do not use only a witness testimony when direct observation is required.

You as the assessor have to judge this evidence to ensure its validity. Therefore you must carry out the following before being able to sign it off as an acceptable piece of evidence.

If you encounter any difficulty in judging the evidence competent/not yet competent then you should write to the Internal Verifier using the Assessors Question Form (**Annex C**).

Valid - Ensure that the comments written relate directly to the Unit/Element to be assessed, so that each Performance Criteria/Range Statement (Scope)/Knowledge Statement you are assessing can clearly be matched.

Authentic - Ensure the witnesses name, location and telephone are recorded on the statement. Check with the witness to confirm they did indeed write/sign the witness statement. Sign and date the witness statement and add the comment "authenticated with witness" to confirm you having authenticated it. Check the witness has been entered on the Witness List in the candidate's portfolio.

Current - Use questioning to confirm some of the areas covered by the statement to ensure that the candidate is still current. Record the question/answers on a question form (**Annex F**). Ensure that witness of performance is from no longer than 3 years before.

Sufficient - Ensure that each Performance Criteria/Range Statement (Scope) /Knowledge Statement that you are assessing can clearly be identified **IN FULL** on the statement. If not then use a question form (**Annex F**) to record any questions you need to ask to supplement the statement to be able to give a full competence decision for each Performance Criteria/Range Statement (Scope)/Knowledge Statement.

Sensitive - Always ensure that no information is recorded that could lead to the identification of specific customers, work colleagues or patients. These people should only be identified only if:

i)   absolutely necessary to validate the evidence.
ii)   the permission of the individual has been sought and obtained.
iii)   They are registered on the Witness List in the candidate's portfolio.

Also ensure no privileged/confidential/restricted information is recorded. If in any doubt always double check with the candidates line management to ensure no breach of the Companies Security Protocols, Data Protection Act / Access to Health Records Act etc.

Product Inspection

This can be used in conjunction with your direct observation, or as a task for the candidate to do between the Assessment Planning Session and the Judgement Session.

Product Inspection is used by an assessor to judge the physical ability of a candidate in producing a piece of work in the normal course of the candidates' work. Whilst almost anything can be used as a Product Inspection you must always be sure that it proves the candidates actual ability to do something. Photocopies of policy letters, blank forms etc do not prove a candidate can do something, so it needs to be something the candidate has completed, produced, made etc and has been used in a real time work situation.

The product should be a copy of the item used in the real time work activity so that it may be entered in the candidates' portfolio. If this is impracticable for any reason such as size etc, then a photograph of the object could be used. Otherwise you would need to enter a written statement as evidence detailing the product, its location and how an Internal or External Verifier could view it.

If you encounter any difficulty in judging the evidence competent/not yet competent then you should write to the Internal Verifier using the Assessors Question Form (**Annex C**).

Valid - Ensure that the product being produced is relevant to the Unit/Element that is being assessed.

Authentic - If you have not physically seen the candidate produce the product then you would have to confirm with someone in the workplace that did see the candidate produce the work. This would be best in the form of a Witness Testimony that could be used in conjunction with the product therefore using 2 pieces of evidence to cover the Performance Criteria/Range Statement (Scope)/Knowledge Statement. If this is not possible then use a question form (**Annex F**) to record questions and answers you need to confirm it was the candidates' own work. The item entered into candidates' portfolio as evidence must have your signature, date and comment "*Authenticated Candidates Own Work*".

Current - A product can be used that has been completed in the past but should be within the last 3 years. However you will need to use a question form (**Annex F**) to record questions and answers you need to confirm that the candidate is still capable of doing the task.

Sufficient - Ensure that each Performance Criteria/Range Statement (Scope) /Knowledge Statement that you are assessing can clearly be identified **IN FULL** from the product. If not then use a question form (**Annex F**) to record any questions you need to ask to supplement the product to be able to give a full competence decision for each Performance Criteria/Range Statement (Scope)/Knowledge Statement.

Sensitive - Always ensure that the product has no information on it that could lead to the identification of specific customers, work colleagues or patients. These people should only be identified only if:

     i)   absolutely necessary to validate the evidence.

     ii)   the permission of the individual has been sought and obtained.

     iii)   They are registered on the Witness List in the candidate's portfolio.

Also ensure the product is not a privileged/confidential/restricted item. If in any doubt always double check with the candidates line management to ensure no breach of the Companies Security Protocols, Data Protection Act / Access to Health Records Act etc.

Project/Assignment

This method of assessment is ideal for using against the knowledge statements. Setting the candidate a project/assignment to produce knowledge evidence shows the candidates true understanding of the Unit being undertaken.

This can then also be used to cover any Performance Criteria/Range Statement (Scope) that is proving difficult to get direct observation for.

Alternatively, you may use specific small assignments to cover Performance Criteria/Range Statements (Scope) that are not routinely undertaken in the workplace.

Always ensure that when setting Projects/Assignments you are happy that the candidate has access to suitable reference material, equipment and support.

If you encounter any difficulty in judging the evidence competent/not yet competent then you should write to the Internal Verifier using the Assessors Question Form (**Annex C**).

Valid - Ensure that the comments written relate directly to the Unit/Element to be assessed, so that each Performance Criteria/Range Statement (Scope)/Knowledge Statement you are assessing can clearly be matched.

Authentic - Ensure the candidates name and the date are recorded on the Project/Assignment. Use a question form (**Annex F**) to record the questions and answers you need to confirm it was the candidates' own work. The Project/Assignment must have your signature, date and comment "*Authenticated Candidates Own Work*".

Current - A Project/Assignment can be used that has been completed in the past but should be within the last 3 years. However you will need to use a question form (**Annex F**) to record questions and answers you need to confirm that the candidate is still capable of doing the task, or having the knowledge.

Sufficient - Ensure that each Performance Criteria/Range Statement (Scope) /Knowledge Statement that you are assessing can clearly be identified **IN FULL** on the Project/Assignment. If not then use a question form (**Annex F**) to record any questions you need to ask to supplement it to be able to give a full competence decision for each Performance Criteria/Range Statement (Scope)/Knowledge Statement.

Sensitive - Always ensure that no information is recorded that could lead to the identification of specific customers, work colleagues or patients. These people should only be identified only if:

      i) absolutely necessary to validate the evidence.
      ii) the permission of the individual has been sought and obtained.
      iii) They are registered on the Witness List in the candidate's portfolio.

Also ensure no privileged/confidential/restricted information is recorded. If in any doubt always double check with the candidates line management to ensure no breach of the Companies Security Protocols, Data Protection Act / Access to Health Records Act etc.

Oral Questions

This method of assessment is best used in support of other methods of assessment to clarify any points or cover any Performance Criteria/Range Statement (Scope)/Knowledge Statements that are proving difficult to provide another type of evidence for.

It is always wise to plan for Oral Questions devised by yourself on every assessment plan, allowing you the opportunity to react to any unplanned events/changes. This will give you a greater chance at being able to give competence decisions.

Even though you are giving the questions orally, you must write down both the question and the answer to be able to use them as evidence. Just saying you questioned someone is not robust enough evidence. Use the question bank form at *(Annex F)*.

If you encounter any difficulty in judging or planning Oral Questions to give competent/not yet competent decisions, then you should write to the Internal Verifier using the Assessors Question Form *(Annex C)*.

Valid - Ensure that the questions used relate directly to the Unit/Element to be assessed, so that each Performance Criteria/Range (Scope) /Knowledge Statement you are assessing can clearly be matched.

Authentic - Ensure the candidates name and the date are recorded on the question form *(Annex F)*. You must remember to put your signature, date and comment "*Authenticated Candidates Own Work*", as well as circling the word oral to indicate these were oral questions.

Current - By using oral questions this will automatically produce evidence that proves the candidate is current in their knowledge and performance.

Sufficient - Ensure that each Performance Criteria/Range Statement (Scope) /Knowledge Statement that you are assessing can clearly be identified *IN FULL* on the Form. You must also indicate if you feel the answer given is correct, do this with a tick. If not place a cross next to it and explain why it is not correct on the Feedback Form. That way each question can be seen why it has/has not been used as evidence.

Sensitive - Always ensure that no information is recorded that could lead to the identification of specific customers, work colleagues or patients. These people should only be identified only if:

       i)   absolutely necessary to validate the evidence.
       ii)   the permission of the individual has been sought and obtained.
       iii)   They are registered on the Witness List in the candidate's portfolio.

Also ensure no privileged/confidential/restricted information is recorded. If in any doubt always double check with the candidates line management to ensure no breach of the Data Protection Act / Access to Health Records Act etc.

Written Questions

These again are best used in support of other methods of assessment to clarify any points or cover any Performance Criteria/Range Statement (Scope)/Knowledge Statements that are proving difficult to provide another type of evidence for.

Again use the question bank form *(Annex F)*.

This way of questioning candidates can be useful as it can be done while you are judging other pieces of evidence, thus saving time.

If you encounter any difficulty in judging or planning Written Questions to give competent /not yet competent decisions, then you should write to the Internal Verifier using the Assessors Question Form (**Annex C**).

Valid - Ensure that the questions used relate directly to the Unit/Element to be assessed, so that each Performance Criteria/Range Statement (Scope)/Knowledge Statement you are assessing can clearly be matched.

Authentic - Ensure the candidates name and the date are recorded on the question form (*Annex F*). If you have set these questions for the candidate to complete when you are not there, you will need to verbally check one or two to be sure in your own mind that it was the candidate that produced the work and knows the subject. Otherwise it could be easy for the candidate just to copy straight out of a book or have had someone else provide the answer for them. You must remember to put your signature, date and comment "*Authenticated Candidates Own Work*", as well as circling the word written to indicate these were written questions.

Current - By using written questions this will automatically produce evidence that is current, providing it has been authenticated properly.

Sufficient - Ensure that each Performance Criteria/Range Statement (Scope) /Knowledge Statement that you are assessing can clearly be identified *IN FULL* on the Form. You must also indicate if you feel the answer given is correct, do this with a tick. If not place a cross next to it and explain why it is not correct on the Feedback Form. That way each question can be seen why it has/has not been used as evidence.

Sensitive - Always ensure that no information is recorded that could lead to the identification of specific customers, work colleagues or patients. These people should only be identified only if:

      i)   absolutely necessary to validate the evidence.
      ii)   the permission of the individual has been sought and obtained.
      iii)   They are registered on the Witness List in the candidate's portfolio.

Also ensure no privileged/confidential/restricted information is recorded. If in any doubt always double check with the candidates line management to ensure no breach of the Data Protection Act / Access to Health Records Act etc.

Accreditation of Prior Learning

Use of candidate's previous qualifications is an excellent way to ensure work is not needlessly repeated. Qualifications must be no older than 3 years, and some questioning will be required to ensure the candidates knowledge is still current.

However great care should be taken to ensure that competence is not given to a candidate because of assumed content of previous qualifications. You will need to satisfy yourself completely that a qualification covers each Performance Criteria/Range Statement (Scope)/Knowledge Statement.

Unless you have access to the exact course content, Instructional Specification or Syllabus then you cannot make a competent decision.

If you encounter any difficulty in judging whether previous qualifications are able to give competent /not yet competent decisions, then you should write to the Internal Verifier using the Assessors Question Form (**Annex C**).

Valid - Ensure that the qualification, or part thereof, relates directly to the Unit/Element to be assessed.

Authentic - Ensure that you see the candidates original certificates, this will ensure that it can be attributed to the candidate. Photocopy the certificate and authenticate the copy by writing the comment "*Certified Original Seen*", then date and sign it.

Current - A Certificate can be used if it has been issued within the last 3 years, when the candidates completed NVQ portfolio is submitted to the NVQ Centre for final certification. However you will need to use a question form (**Annex F**) to record questions and answers you need to confirm that the candidate is still capable of doing the task, or having the knowledge.

Sufficient - Ensure that each Performance Criteria/Range Statement (Scope) /Knowledge Statement that you are assessing can clearly be identified **IN FULL** from the course content, Instructional Specification or Syllabus. If not then use a question form (**Annex F**) to record any questions you need to ask to supplement the certificate to be able to give a full competence decision for each Performance Criteria/Range Statement (Scope)/Knowledge Statement. Be aware of what type of qualification is being accredited, if it is an Academic qualification that had no practical assessment, then it may only be used for Knowledge Statements. If it is a qualification that was examined or tested for practical ability, then it may be used for Performance Criteria, Range Statements (Scope) and Knowledge Statements.

Sensitive - Always ensure that no information is recorded that could lead to the identification of specific customers, work colleagues or patients. These people should only be identified only if:

      i)   absolutely necessary to validate the evidence.

      ii)   the permission of the individual has been sought and obtained.

      iii)   They are registered on the Witness List in the candidate's portfolio.

Also ensure no privileged/confidential/restricted information is recorded. If in any doubt always double check with the candidates line management to ensure no breach of the Data Protection Act / Access to Health Records Act etc.

Naturally Occurring

Naturally Occurring Evidence is not an assessment method in its own right. It is in fact an indicator as to whether the method of assessment used was judging a candidate's actual performance on the job.

It is used to highlight whether the candidates evidence was generated during normal daily work activities. Therefore if you have chosen methods of assessing your candidate that produce evidence during their normal work activities, then delete simulation in the in the Naturally Occurring/Simulation box on the assessment plan.

Simulation

Simulation is not an assessment method in its own right. It is in fact an indicator as to whether the methods of assessment used to judge a candidate's performance were a simulated scenario or task, because Naturally Occurring Evidence was not available. A good example of this would be Basic Life Support (CPR).

Therefore if you have chosen methods of assessing your candidate that produce evidence from situations specifically set up for the purpose of NVQ Assessment, then delete Naturally Occurring in the in the Naturally Simulation/Simulation box on the assessment plan

Using Simulation should only be considered if naturally occurring evidence is not available, or if specifically asked for in the evidence requirements.

Simulation has very tight controls on its use, due to trying to ensure equal, fair and reliable assessment to all students registered in the centre.

The primary concern with using Simulation is that *"It must be as near to the real situation as is reasonably practicable"*. Because of this there is a Simulation Log held in the centre to ensure that if a simulation is used for any part of a qualification, it is always administered the same way for all candidates.

Therefore if you wish to use Simulation you must complete the Simulation Authority Request Form at *Annex J*, and forward it to the Internal Verifier. The Internal Verifier will then inform you of how the simulation will have to be administered.

© Piers Liron

Particular Assessment Requirements (PAR)

Particular Assessment Requirements, or Special Assessment Requirements as they are sometimes known, is something that prevents the assessor carrying out an assessment of a candidate in the way the assessor would normally do so.

It can be a circumstance that causes difficulties in carrying out an assessment such as:

    a.   The assessor and candidate do not work at the same location.

    b.   The assessor and candidate do not work on the same shift.

It could also be that the candidate has a situation that would not allow the assessor to carry out an assessment in a normal manner, such as:

    a.   <u>A physical disability or impairment</u>. This could be either permanent resulting from, for instance, spina bifida, paraplegia or temporary incapacities such as a broken arm. Arrangements could be made for the use of a writer, mechanical/electronic aids or extra time allowed in examinations.

    b.   <u>A hearing impairment</u>. Arrangements could include the use of a communicator/interpreter (sign language), mechanical or electronic aids or extra time.

    c.   <u>A visual impairment</u>. Arrangements could include the use of a writer, a reader, tapes, question papers with large print, Braille or moon, use of a keyboard to produce typescript answers or extra time.

    d.   <u>A learning difficulty</u>. Candidates with a learning difficulty should be able to identify there specific needs at your initial interview with them. If the candidate has undergone a diagnosis with an educational psychologist they will have a report specifying their individual needs. This could be a requirement to have written work a certain size, typed in a specific font such as comic sans MS, or use of certain coloured paper.

        Should you suspect a candidate has a learning difficulty, such as reading, writing or numerical problems then you should seek guidance from the Internal Verifier immediately.

        Arrangements could be made for the candidate to use video/audio cassette tapes as evidence instead of written work.

    e.   <u>Medical conditions</u>. Where a candidate has a diagnosed medical condition such as epilepsy, diabetes or respiratory disorders individual cases should be considered on their merit with the Internal Verifier.

To ensure the NVQ Centre is offering all its candidates the right to fair and reliable assessment, *any* situation that either causes or has the potential to cause difficulties in carrying out assessment, must be notified to the Internal Verifier *immediately* by using the **PAR Request Form at *Annex B*.**

This allows the NVQ Centre to ensure the same solutions are used for everyone having the same difficulty in assessing.

You will need:

1 x PAR Request Form at *Annex B*

Procedure:

1.   Fill in your name as the assessor and add the date. Then fill in the name of the candidate and their Awarding Body Enrolment Number *(found on their enrolment form)*

2.   Give as full a description of the problem as you can, indicating what would prevent a fair, reliable or timely assessment to take place.

3.   Forward this to your Internal Verifier as soon as possible.

4.   The Internal Verifier will contact you to discuss the matter, and agree with you a suitable course of action to take. A written reply will follow shortly thereafter.

5.   Place a copy of this in your assessor file and also a copy in the candidates portfolio.

6.   Assess the candidate as guided by the returned PAR Form.

Assessor Questions

Should you need to ask a question of the Internal Verifier you should always submit it in writing using the form at *Annex C*.

Your question could be for help in interpreting a performance criterion, range/scope or knowledge statement. It could also be to clarify exactly what is required to meet one of these or exactly what evidence must be used.

This allows the question to be registered in the Assessors Question Log and the answer fed back not only to yourself but to all the other assessors as well through the centres assessor standardisation meetings. This enables the NVQ Centre to ensure equality in assessment for all candidates.

You will need:

1 x Assessor Question Form (*Annex C*)

Procedure:

1.   Fill in your name and the title of the NVQ you are assessing, then sign and date in the appropriate boxes.

2.   Fully explain your query/question/concern in the box provided, if you feel you have a suggestion or your interpretation then include this as well.

3.   Send it immediately to the Internal Verifier who will provide you with the answer you require.

4.   Once you have received the reply from the Internal Verifier you can then go ahead and assess the candidate as directed.

Candidate Appeals Procedure

Candidates have the right to challenge either an assessor's plan for assessment or the assessment decision made by an assessor on a unit of competence.

Assessor's must assist a candidate in using the appeals procedure and should offer the process to a candidate when a face-to-face meeting fails to resolve any issues the candidate may have.

It should not be taken personally but instead be used to clarify any points to ensure that fair and reliable assessment has taken place.

You will need:

1 x Candidate Appeals Form (*Annex G*)

Procedure:

1.   The candidate should first discuss the reason for appeal with the Assessor if at all possible.

2.   If the candidate is not satisfied with the Assessors final decision an appeal should be made using the Candidates Appeals Form (*Annex G*).

3.   Complete the Candidates, Assessors and Internal Verifiers boxes with the relevant names.

4.   In the date of assessment box put the date on which the assessment planning session or actual assessment took place where the candidate disagrees.

5.   Put the Unit number and name in the Units assessed box.

6.   Photocopy the Assessment Plan, and NVQ Review Form if the assessment took place, and attach them to the Candidates Appeals Form.

7.   The candidate should then detail their reason for the appeal in the first box, then date and sign in the relevant boxes.

8.   The Assessor should then detail their reason for their assessment decision, then date and sign in the relevant box.

9.   The Candidate Appeals Form should then be forwarded to the Internal Verifier Immediately. The Internal Verifier will then complete their box and forward their decision to the Assessor. You will then need to give this to the candidate as soon as possible and discuss the Internal Verifiers decision.

10.   The assessment should then take place as directed by the Internal Verifier, or the assessment decision amended or upheld as directed.

11.   If the candidate is not satisfied with the findings of the Internal Verifier, the candidate should complete the comments box on the Internal Verifiers decision and forward this back to the Internal Verifier via the Assessor.

12.   This will be forwarded to the External Verifier by the Internal Verifier. The External Verifier will examine the evidence and notify the Internal Verifier, Assessor and Candidate by completing the External Verifiers comments/decision box.

13.   The External Verifiers decision is final and the assessment should then take place as directed, or the decision amended or let stand as directed.

Note
Comprehensive records are made of any appeal and subsequent actions and findings in line with City and Guilds Publication 'Providing City & Guilds Qualifications' Section 7 and the NVQ Code of Practice.

Simulation Request

Should you need to use simulation to gather evidence from your candidate you must ask for authority from the Internal Verifier, this must always be submitted it in writing using the form at *Annex J*.

This allows the simulation to be registered in the Simulation Log and the answer fed back not only to yourself but to all the other assessors as well through the centres assessor standardisation meetings. This enables the NVQ Centre to ensure equality in assessment for all candidates.

You will need:

1 x Simulation Authority Request Form (*Annex J*)

Procedure:

1.   Fill in your name, date and the title of the NVQ you are assessing, then enter the exact Unit/Element.

2.   Fully detail the simulation you are wishing to use in the box provided, including equipment/location/timings/people involved etc.

3.   Send it immediately to the Internal Verifier for approval. This will either be given or the Internal Verifier will provide exact details of how the simulation should be carried out.

4.   Once you have received the reply from the Internal Verifier you can then go ahead and assess the candidate using the simulation as directed.

Intentionally Blank

CANDIDATE INITIAL INTERVIEW

NVQ Qualifications And/Or Experience	
Other Qualifications Relevant to NVQ	
Prior/Current Experience Relevant to NVQ	
Particular or Special Assessment Requirements	
	PAR Form Raised - Yes / No

This information should now be used to aid your Assessment planning with the candidate, i.e. which units to attempt first. Each assessment plan should be signed and agreed by you and the candidate.

Candidates Signature		Assessors signature	
Candidates Name		Assessors Name	
Date		Date	

Intentionally Blank

PAR Register No:

PARTICULAR ASSESSMENT REQUIREMENT REQUEST FORM

Assessor Name:		**Date:**	
Candidate Name:		**Awarding Body Enrolment No:**	

Description of Requirements/Situations:

Candidates Signature		**Assessors signature**	
Date		**Date**	

Solution to Requirements/Situations from Internal Verifier:

IV Name		Sig		Date	
Review Date:		Date Review Took Place:			

ANNEX C

Question Register No:

ASSESSORS QUESTIONS FORM

Assessor Name		NVQ Title	
Signature		Date	

Question/Query/Concern/Clarification required. Enter as much detail as possible- including your interpretation and or suggested solution.

Internal Verifier Comments and decision.

Signature		Date	
IV Name			

Tick to indicate type		ASSESSMENT PLAN	No	
Initial	Review			

Candidate's Name:		Assessor Name:	
Qualification:		Units:	

Enter Element No, PC's, Range &/or Evidence Requirements:		*Delete as applicable Naturally Occurring /Simulated*

When & Where you will Assess/Review

Date:		Time:		Location:	

Does the candidate have a PAR?	Yes	No	If yes, specify the PAR No. allocated by the Centre.	

Method of Assessment Indicate below in the left hand column by inserting a ✔, the method chosen	Evidence to be provided Identify here the items of evidence to be collected, not the methods. Indicate with a ✔ in the right hand column if the evidence is of a sensitive nature/confidential.	
Observation		
Product Inspection		
Oral Questions		
Written Questions		
Witness Testimony		
Project/Assignment		
APL		
Other		
Details of those people involved in the assessment process other than the Assessor & Candidate.		

Details of how Confidential Information or Sensitive Issues will be dealt with:

Candidates Signature		Assessors Signature	
Date		Date	

NVQ Review / Feedback Sheet
Remarks:

Assessors Signature			
Candidates Signature			
Date feedback given		**Date Planned for Review**	

Tick to indicate type	
Initial	Review
✓	

ASSESSMENT PLAN

No | 5

Candidate's Name:	JOE BLOGGS	Assessor Name:	ANN SMITH
Qualification:	Oral Health Care Dental Nurse	Units:	DN21

Enter Element No, PC's, Range &/or Evidence Requirements:	DN21.1 All PCs All Ranges DN21.2 PCs 1 – 7 All Ranges DN21 All Knowledge Statements	*Delete as applicable Naturally Occurring /Simulated*

When & Where you will Assess/Review

Date:	22/3/03	Time:	0900	Location:	Keogh Dental Centre – Surgery 1

Does the candidate have a PAR?	~~Yes~~	No	If yes, specify the PAR No. allocated by the Centre.	N/A

Method of Assessment		Evidence to be provided	
Indicate below in the left hand column by inserting a ✓, the method chosen		Identify here the items of evidence to be collected, not the methods. Indicate with a ✓ in the right hand column if the evidence is of a sensitive nature/confidential.	
✓	Observation	Of setting up surgery & assisting during endodontic appt	✓
	Product Inspection		
✓	Oral Questions	Devised by assessor as required	
✓	Written Questions	Completed knowledge questions given today	
	Witness Testimony		
	Project/Assignment		
	APL		
	Other		

Details of those people involved in the assessment process other than the Assessor & Candidate.	Garth Brooks BDS, Dental Centre Keogh, Tel 01252 96969696
	Patient receiving endodontic treatment

Details of how Confidential Information or Sensitive Issues will be dealt with:

The patient receiving the endodontic appointment will be asked for their permission to allow the observation during the appointment to take place. The patient will be informed that no details will be recorded that will allow them to be identified to ensure patient confidentiality is maintained.

Candidates Signature	**Joe Bloggs**	Assessors Signature	Ann Smith
Date	15/3/03	Date	15/3/03

NVQ Review / Feedback Sheet

Remarks:

Joe, well done on todays assessment. I was pleased we managed to get so much done towards this unit, however we did not achieve all we had planed to today. I can now give the following competence from the evidence produced today:

Observation Report

DN21.1
Competent Performance Criteria 1, 2, 3, 4, 5, 6, 7, 8, 9, 10, 11, Range Statement 1a
Not yet competent for Performance Criteria 12 – this was due to it not being observed, however an oral question was asked to cover this.
Not yet competent for Range Statements 1b-1e – this was due to only root canal treatment being observed.

DN21.2
Competent All Performance Criteria, Range Statement 1a
Not yet competent for Range Statements 1b – this was due to only root canal treatment being observed.

Written Questions

DN21 Knowledge Statements
Competent for Knowledge Statements 1 – 46
Not yet competent for Knowledge Statements 47 – 54, this is due to you not having completed the questions that I set you from the question bank.

Oral Questions

DN21.1
Competent for Performance Criteria 12

Please now insert the observation form, your written answers sheet and the oral question/answer sheet into the evidence section of your NVQ Portfolio and cross-refer them to the evidence profile sheets for unit DN21.

We now just need to plan an assessment to observe the remaining Range Statements and judge the remaining written questions for the Knowledge Statements when you have completed them. Well done on achieving the above competence today, lets plan to do the rest of this unit by the 10/4/03 so we can sign this unit off.

Assessors Signature	*Ann Smith*		
Candidates Signature	**Joe Bloggs**		
Date feedback given	*15/3/03*	**Date Planned for Review**	*10/4/03*

PTO

Unit:	

Question/Answer Sheet

Question No.	
	Question
1	
	Answer
Oral/Written	
	Question
2	
	Answer
Oral/Written	

Question No.	
3 Oral/Written	**Question**
	Answer
4 Oral/Written	**Question**
	Answer

Candidates Signature		Assessors signature	
Candidates Name		Assessors Name	
Date		Date	

Annex G

CANDIDATES APPEALS FORM

Register No:

Candidates Name	
Assessors Name	
Internal verifiers Name	
Date of assessment	
Unit/s assessed	
Copy of Assessment plan attached	

Candidates reason for appeal (Copy of assessment plan attached)

Candidates Signature		Date:	

Assessors Comments/Assessment details

Assessors Signature		Date:	

Internal Verifiers Comments/Decision

Date appeal received:		Date of reply:	
IV Name		Signature	

Candidates Comments if not happy with IV decision

Candidate Signature		Date:	

External Verifiers Comments/Decision

Date appeal received:		Date of reply:	
EV Name		Signature	

OBSERVATION REPORT

Evidence Number:

Task:	
Elements:	

Candidate Name:	
Assessor Name:	
Date of Observation:	

Today I observed the candidate:

Initials

1. _____

_____

2. _____

_____

3. _____

_____

4. _____

_____

5. _____

_____

6. _____

_____

7. _____

_____

Don't forget to expand on these comments in the feedback box below.

Feedback/comments:

	Name	Signature	Date of Feedback
Candidate			
Assessor			

EVIDENCE PROFILE SHEET

Unit No.	DN14	Element No	DN14.2
Candidates name			

PC Ref	EVIDENCE	Refer to Evidence No
1	Written Questions	2
2	Observation Report	1
3	Written Questions	2
4	Observation Report	1
5	Written Questions	2
6	Written Questions	2
7	Written Questions	2
8	Observation Report	1
9	Observation Report	1
10		
11	Observation Report	1
12	Observation Report	1
Range Statements	Evidence Description	Evidence Reference(s)
1a	Written Questions	2
1b	Observation Report	1
1c	Written Questions	2
2a	Observation Report	1
2b	Written Questions	2

Methods of assessment	Observation of performance*	Inspection of product*	Questioning*
* delete as required	Simulations*	Accreditation of Prior Learning/Experience*	Project/Assignment*

Assessors name	Assessors signature	Date

IV name	IV signature	Date

Intentionally Blank

ANNEX J

SAR No:

SIMULATION AUTHORITY REQUEST FORM

Assessor Name:		Date:	
NVQ Title		Unit/Element	

Description of Requirements/Simulations:

Solution to Requirements/Simulations from Internal Verifier:

NOT AUTHORISED / AUTHORISED

IV Name		Sig		Date	
Review Date:		Date Review Took Place:			

Intentionally Blank